Vs.

BY THE SAME AUTHOR
The Sleeping Life

Vs.

Kerry Ryan

ANVIL PRESS • VANCOUVER • 2010

Copyright © 2010 by Kerry Ryan

Anvil Press Inc.
P.O. Box 3008, Main Post Office
Vancouver, B.C. V6B 3X5 CANADA
www.anvilpress.com

First Printing.

All rights reserved. No part of this book may be reproduced by any means without the prior written permission of the publisher, with the exception of brief passages in reviews. Any request for photocopying or other reprographic copying of any part of this book must be directed in writing to ACCESS: The Canadian Copyright Licensing Agency, One Yonge Street, Suite 800, Toronto, Ontario, Canada, M5E 1E5.

Library and Archives Canada Cataloguing in Publication

Ryan, Kerry, 1975-
  Vs. / Kerry Ryan.

Poems.
ISBN 978-1-897535-34-9

  1. Boxing--Poetry. I. Title.

PS8635.Y356V47 2010   C811'.6   C2010-906298-1

Printed and bound in Canada
Cover design: Jeope Wolfe
Cover image: "The Bennett Sisters" (Courtesy of Wikimedia Commons)
Interior design: HeimatHouse

Represented in Canada by the Literary Press Group
Distributed by the University of Toronto Press

The publisher gratefully acknowledges the financial assistance of the Canada Council for the Arts, the Canada Book Fund, the Province of British Columbia through the BC Arts Council and the Book Publishing Tax Credit.

For Jeope, for always being in my corner.

CONTENTS

Bloodline 9

WHY
Jab 13
No Good Reason 14
Careful 15
Boxing Club 16
Champ 18
Tentative 20
Fight Card 21

TRAINING
Cross 25
Wrap 26
Theory 27
Playground 28
Medicine Ball 29
Focus Gloves 30
Roadwork 31
Heavy Bag 32
Shadow Box 34
Stretch 35

IN THE RING
One-two 39
Gloved 40
Warm Up 41
First Time in the Ring 42
The Hardest Lesson 44
Retraining 45
Unresponsive 46
Excuses 47
Defensive 49
The Difference 50

Sweat 51
Tell 52
Staging 53
Throat 54
Breather 55
Sparring Partner 56
Trickster 58
Insatiable 59
Imprint 60
Ribbing 61

FIGHTING
Hook 65
Dinner Conversation 66
Natural 67
Defeat 68
Falter 69
Tender 70
Toast 71
Matched 72
Friday Night Fights 73
Expectation 74
Muscle 76
Photo 77

SIX MINUTES
Uppercut 81
Dual/duel 82
Weight Class 85
Commitment 86
Locker Room 87
Silence 88
Six Minutes 89
Win 92
Replay 93
Naming 94
After 95

"A boxer, like a writer, must stand alone."

— A.J. Liebling, *The Sweet Science*

bloodline

Dad turns my trophy in his hands,
tells me about the one he earned
a long-lost summer camp memento,
a story I've never heard

I didn't know
boxing ran in the family,
along with other rough habits,
pooled in generations of lanky uncles

I ask if he wore headgear, mouthguard,
as if I'd scold him now, or his grinning
black and white photo at age nine

Ask about black eyes, loose teeth,
winner or loser but all he remembers
is his introduction, intact to the word:

> *The Winnipeg Walloper*
> *Manitoba Mauler*
> *Canadian Clubber*

He must have repeated it to himself
every night in his bunk,
the announcer's faith in his strength
seeping into muscle

That prize lasts a lifetime
not on a mantel,
but rooted in the body,
lighting it quietly from the inside

WHY

jab

*Shoulder snaps whip of muscle
live wire licking Everlast emblem
stamps out sparks*

*Leather sizzles
reignites*

no good reason

I have no score to settle,
nothing to prove through fists
no child to inspire, snub to avenge

I watch documentaries
on Ali for the poetry,
Raging Bull on a De Niro kick

I've never dreamt
of blood on my knuckles,
eyes stuffed with bruise

I'm bookish, shy,
keep the red gloves
under my desk

When someone asks
how I square
my careful nature
with punches
the best I can think of is
for the hell of it

But that doesn't have
the muscle, stamina
to protect me from blows,
the sudden thunder of panic

careful

I test batteries
in every smoke detector
check and recheck
locked doors, cold ovens

I'd never trade sure footing
for a dazzling view
from a dangerous edge
or bike helmet
for wind in my hair

So I'm surprised
to find myself
in the line of a fist
with its terrible possibilities

And shocked to discover
that the ache of risk
is so delicious

boxing club

This is not the library
not a coffee shop or movie theatre
not any place I belong

It's a cliché, the grimy set
of a grainy black and white film

Slick biceps
mashed noses
drenched muscle shirts

Dingy reek of sweat and old leather
heavy bags sway
with the memory of pounding

Staccato smack:
knuckle on focus glove,
medicine ball in gut,
skipping rope on stained canvas

But someone smiles—
red face twinkling—
and I decide to stay
five more minutes

Notice the unicorn tattoo
on a thick shoulder,
butterfly sticker glittering
on bulb of bag glove

Coach's *you can do this*
dries on my ear

champ

His clippings brittle
on the brick wall, yellowing
with La Motta, Dempsey, Louis

He checks memberships in the club
just like the one he trained in
decades ago, between bouts
north in logging camps

Sweatpants over gut,
three-days' beard
around his smile,
says the same line
every time he sees me:
I feel safe now that you're here

I forget how close
he's lived to danger—saws, fists
how different that is
from a lunch-hour boxing lesson

Behind the desk, his fingers thick
on small calculator keys,
shyly neatening bills in the cashbox
but you can see how comfortably
they'd curl into boxing gloves

(His handwriting a shock:
proper and finely-looped
as a schoolteacher's)

In the gym he holds heavy bags
as casually as you might slip hands
around a lover's waist

He can't tell you how to throw a hook,
how to crowd the bag
close enough to clinch,
forehead almost resting on leather
how a sudden twist wrings out waist,
lights a fuse that explodes in the bag's ear

He explains with a perfect tight arc,
one word: *bam*
hands teach everything
he's learned with his body

I know it's only those old blows
that keep his mind
from making a fist around my name,
but I still flicker pride
every time he calls me *champ*

tentative

A fight is fragile
threat of broken bone,
shattered courage,
change in weight or heart

It's theory to be proven
only with a tap of gloves

But a boxer has to train
as if it's certain
build muscle
believing it'll be used

Keep mind loose, limber
write the word *if*
in a square on the calendar

fight card

Never imagined
my name on a fight card
the way I did
a book cover

But delight
buzzes brighter
seeing those
familiar letters
threaded together
so far from where
they're expected

TRAINING

cross

Arm a battering ram
drills hard, certain
relentless as a machine
fed on guts, new muscle

wrap

Slow your mind
to the ritual
of preparing hands

Wind strip of red cotton
around thumb, wrist,
bury wedding band

Cat's cradle extra passes
over scuffed knuckle

Criss-cross
criss-cross
criss-cross

Rhythm of the one-two
coming into your breath

theory

Trainer barks *hands up*—
more bank robbery
than heavy bag drill—
threatens a lifetime of push-ups

And you know,
       you know,
              you know
why your hands can't sleep,
can't slip from your chin

But you're not in the ring,
the bag doesn't hit back
and the weight
and heat of gloves
is enough to drag knuckles
to the floor

This is your first fight:
holding fists to your jaw

Your fiercest opponents:
exhaustion, gravity

playground

All those awkward years
you didn't realize you were training

Miss Mary Mack, Mack, Mack
clapped fast, fast, faster
to the recess bell
now it's whip-sharp palm-sting
of focus gloves,
flat leather slaps blurring

Not the school wall
that absorbs the bounce
but your partner's gut,
then yours—
hauling medicine ball,
shoving breath from lungs

No pink plastic double dutch ropes,
little girl nonsense songs,
only heavy metal
as you slice air
rope bites floor
quick as ticks of stopwatch
Fast as blood
pulsing through temples

medicine ball

It doesn't matter that you're a woman—
delicate belly, fragile confidence

You lace gut tight,
breathe sharp through teeth
catch—hard as a sack of dirt,
crack of baseball bat—
in the tender muscle
that slings between ribs, pelvis

Medicine ball a full-term pregnancy
you heave back and forth
with your partner
teaches you how to take a blow
without folding double,
how to live with ache
in the centre of your body

focus gloves

Partner calls punches
your arms unspool
bolts of pale cord
from your shoulders
recoil fast
as night crawlers
into dark earth

You're awed
by the taut pop—
prong licking socket—
the secret length
your arms have kept
from you so many years

roadwork

The sweet simplicity of running:

>   feet
>   forward

Breath so smooth, silent
your lungs seem oiled
your body lighter
on concrete than canvas
no one chases you

Sidewalk your heavy bag,
soles punch easy one-twos for miles
before toes bleed

heavy bag

Gloved knuckle
like flint on leather

Jab   jab   jabjab

jabjab

jabjab

CROSS

Machine-accurate,
bolt through the bag

CROSS

CROSS

(breathe)

Clean, heavy:
CROSS

Fist-flicker,
slick, distant kisses
jabCROSS
jabCROSS
jabCROSS

Fire feeds on muscle,
spreads every throw

jab　　　*jab*　　　　　　*jab*

flame rages, arm stumbles, stutters

　　　　　　　　　　jab

　　　　jab　*jab*

CROSS

　　　　Cross

　　　　　　　cross

Right arm rusts through

Left already ash

shadow box

Stare yourself down
in the mirror

Chin tucked out of reach,
right eyebrow twisted up,
taunting

Breath explodes fierce
between teeth

Storm of punches,
straight and long,
blots out your own face

You throw and throw,
pitiless
until reflection pauses,
breathes hard, ragged
and you think
now I've got her on the ropes

stretch

Grab feet, roll chest over knees
until you're a fist
throbbing with breath
wait for heart to slow
its flurry against ribs
Pull shoulders apart
across your back

Let every punch you've thrown
drain to the floor,
pool with sweat from your hair,
the need to prove
the power of your body

IN THE RING

one-two

*Flashbulb of jab
dazes, opens door
for a cross
to storm through*

Demolish

gloved

Shove a wrapped hand
deep into leather,
hook fingers into dead-end
of glove braced
in coach's belly
soft, slow dig to her gut
as she knots laces
around your forearms

Tied and taped, you can't pat
sweat from your face,
flick hair from eyes

Gloves turn hands dumb,
useless except for hammering
a nose flush with cheekbone,
knocking on a forehead
as if testing—stud or hollow

Between rounds you beg for water
to be poured into your mouth
tip your head back, swallow

warm up

Keep arms so long, loose,
they flap with every breath
of ceiling fan

Don't let your T-shirt cool
or sweat dry
along your spine

Constantly prod muscle,
like keeping a concussion awake

Pace miles toe to toe,
inching inside your stance
forward/back
forward/back
rev, ready,
hover over the gas

Pester the mirror
with half-punches
fingers fly open,
fists in full bloom
light but firm,
as if shaking someone
from the strangest dream

first time in the ring

Coach says *throw at my shoulder*
the lump of bared muscle
less human than her face, belly

She hums electric,
her body perfectly tuned,
biceps trying to hatch from skin

She could drop you to the mat, easy,
even though you have thirty pounds on her

Your fists don't want to hit
jab hesitates, sticks on air
like it's asking a question
right hand falls short
even when she doesn't move

She tags your arms, ribs
light, just to show you
how to be hit,
the jolt of it

Tears rise, blur
just like that nightmare:
you can't say *stop*
can only play dead,
hope she'll move on

But she paws at you,
snaps a jab on your forehead
hardly enough to crack an egg,
but it shatters your shyness,
wakes your fists

the hardest lesson

Your fists stall, rear
approaching her face

You have to learn to hit

To watch your glove smash
against her forehead
like a fender into flesh

Have to practice to land
a pure shot to her belly—
hard leather echo—
without saying *sorry*

retraining

Don't flinch
as her knuckles fly in close
search your face
for a spot to land

Don't twist chin away
or turn from the punch
as is your habit
with every unkindness
thrown your direction

Don't ever blink
hold lids steady
even as her glove
fits into your eye socket
dries cornea

unresponsive

You always thought
survival instinct was a given
dormant reflex
deep inside muscle,
a red telephone
awaiting the call

But in the ring you realize
it doesn't come standard
you must decide:
defend/fight
run/hide

Fists swarm your face
you don't even try
to shoo them away
just wait, wonder
what happens next

excuses

Because you never had a brother
or after-school scraps,
carpet burn in the rec room

> You don't know how to hit, be hit
> don't know how to be ruthless

Because you spent those clumsy hours
of high school gym class
trying to be invisible
in sour, wrinkled shorts

> You didn't understand that *sport*
> means setting a destination
> in distant hills, building the road
> then pushing further, roaring past

Because you've always run
at a right angle
from oncoming arguments

> You've learned speed, endurance
> but not how to stand,
> take fear in the face without blinking

Because you've read too many books
in the dim of late evening, early morning,
not wanting to wake
your lover with the lamp

> You can't see the punch
> coiled heavy and hard
> inside the glove

defensive

Your punch is sluggish
as a smart retort to your tongue,
your slip so slow
it makes you laugh

Hunkered behind forearms,
you filter punches with your hands,
gloves staggering back
into cheek and teeth

It's just like a schoolyard bully
or older sister grabbing wrists,
forcing your lame hands
into your own face and asking
why're ya hitting yourself?

You still can't answer
pain worst at your own hand,
the round eternal

the difference

Gloves pop
off leather:
heavy bag, focus glove, headgear

Snap back to cheek,
momentum mounting
arms eager, primed

But flesh grabs and holds,
sucks strength, snuffs energy

Belly swallows your fist,
tugs as you try to reel it in
you catch a handful of jabs
on the forehead
before you can retract
your glove from her gut

sweat

You're used to the heavy bag
waiting patient
for you to blot your face

But in the ring
even a quick swipe,
T-shirt across forehead,
signals her fist:
vulnerable

So you breathe sweat,
swallow it

Let it stream from your face

Drink it, blink it,
wince at its sting

tell

You lean over the café table,
tell a friend you're training
whisper to soften the punches
she'll imagine, but she grins, claps hands

You don't mean to tell
your mother-in-law, but it slips
on a long distance Sunday afternoon
you sense her palm lifting to lips

You won't tell your own nervous mother
until it's a story: past tense, happy ending
know her worry is more powerful
than punches, more corrosive to courage

In the ring, your tell:
slight sag of left fist divulges
the punch, opens your face
invites a glove in

staging

Play your character wily, tough
hit your mark on the canvas,
begin the dialogue of fists—
breath heavily accented with pain

Your cues

Throat withers:
swallow

Gloves flood face:
block

Lungs clench:
breathe

Calf brushes rope:
move

Confidence inflates:
jab

Forehead emerges:
one-two

Thirty-second bell,
falling curtain,
the only line you remember
is *throw*

And *throw* and *throw*

throat

Watch the twinned ridges
of gristle twitching
with every strained breath

Never look at gloves
or she'll get you like a pickpocket:
the left distracting with magic and jabs
while the right sneaks in, ransacks

Read next punch
in the shadow of clavicle

Don't let her eyes hook yours,
drown your resolve
in reedy undertow

Lock onto her heaving collar,
throw six inches north or south
look at her nose, chin,
only with the steady leather attention
of your unflinching fists

breather

She rests
gloves against cheeks,
eyes white-wide
from pulling miles
of new air through nostrils

You should attack,
jam punches
into every open space on her body
but you haven't trained
to be cruel

Give her one unfettered breath,
then shatter it

sparring partner

Grey shirt soaked black
slapped heavy
against his chest
he comes in close,
confides he's tired,
wants you to free your hands—
birds from a cage—
on his face and ribs

He's been an hour
in the ring
every two minutes
a new, uncertain challenger—
skittish with nerves,
draining energy on air

Gently, he unravels each one,
invisible fists light to their foreheads
the lesson: *watch, move*

He slips easily
from your lumbering right,
but lets you back him
to the ropes,
opens his chest
as if taking off a jacket

Words catch on his mouthguard
come get me

You let your hands fly,
but punches soften
into his belly,
jabs so delicate
you might be brushing hair
from his eyes

Close enough to know his nose
is five degrees off plumb,
you don't see his fist
just feel it
crash into your ear

trickster

Thin wick of adrenalin
runs through spent muscle
grin held in place with mouthguard
as you fold out of the ring
victory just lasting a round with him

You watch him with the others
eyes hard as metal washers,
he carefully calibrates speed,
strength, to each opponent
an economy of energy

He shape-shifts with each one:
brick wall
horsefly
feral tom
coy stranger, impossible to reach

When he faces a woman
you see him change:
puppy dog, chew toy
his eyes flannel-soft,
punches diluted, playful

You realize that in the ring
you were not a superhero
stopping a tornado with your hands
that the triumph still dampening your hair
was just a con to build courage,
introduce you to pride

insatiable

Even one round of sparring
punches a hole
in your gut
big as a loaf of bread

Plants a hunger that jabs
inside your ribs
all day, all night

imprint

Your body sorts and stores
every moment in the ring,
tallies punches in columns:
thrown, eaten

Jabs ricochet through your arms
as you haul grocery bags,
lift a glass of water
a fist crumples your belly
every time you laugh

Ache a snug jacket
you wear constantly,
tearing seams along ribs,
across shoulders

Pain crawls into your skull,
takes root and nags
you're too slow, too slow

ribbing

Hours after, her glove still pries
your ribs apart,
clenches lung, twists

You whimper in the bed,
wake with every breath,
shudder at the lapse
that left you prone
to the boulder of her right

Days later, clinic waiting room,
each breath a thimbleful of air,
you press palms against ribcage,
try to contain the fury of a sneeze
ask when you can go
back in the ring

FIGHTING

hook

*Choke air
in the tight angle of elbow*

*Wrench gut, crank spine
crooked arm takes sly, swift
bite of leather*

dinner conversation

I tell you I want to fight
even though it's still a nascent thought
sparkling under ribs—
just to test its strength
in the volley of our voices

But you agree too easily
so I lob the question back
from different angles

Maybe I want you to lash
at the idea, protect me
or maybe I want you
as my first opponent,
the dining room table our ring

But you've thrown the bout
I'm stunned at your trust
in my quivering decision
to stoop between ropes,
commit to bruising

natural

You've never nagged a heavy bag,
won't even try a chin-up
or hoisting a medicine ball
like Atlas and jogging around the gym

But when you lie back,
lace hands casual behind your head,
easy muscle knots your shoulder to elbow
my arms carp, sigh with jealousy
at the cheap strength
that comes naturally to you

defeat

The lid on the strawberry jam
doesn't care
how many rounds
I can go in the ring,
how many push-ups I can shove
into the floor,
how straight and fast my jab,
how adamant my cross

I won't take the jar to you,
can't watch you ease it open
as you sit in front of the TV
so I eat my toast
plain, dry, shameful

falter

After rounds of floundering,
the heat of the house,
your cheery curiosity,
steam out all the tears
I gamely swallowed in the ring
my jacket soaked
before I can unzip it

You look for the wound
but there's no blood
with such a deep gash
to courage

Every reason to quit
dribbles from my slack lips,
muscle begs permission to slump

Your gentle encouragement
only makes me want
to drill a mittened fist
into your unguarded belly

tender

Rib squawks at touch, screams
with every little shift in bed

A tantrum
when I try to turn
toward you

I'm fragile tonight
and you, afraid of crushing me
hold my body
with the heat of your skin

toast

Both wine glasses
locked in the cupboard now
their howling mouths hidden,
but I can hear them, whining *not fair*
like kids sent to bed early,
afraid of the dark

I grumble at tumblers of water
instead of thanking you
for your dry solidarity

You turn coach,
all pep talk, bright sides
tuck knuckles, bump my fist
above the dinner plates,
say *cheers*

matched

We never fight
both youngest children
still wanting to please, appease,
who learned early small never wins
that injury, injustice
fuel poems and pictures,
our different victories

We never compete
except in Scrabble
or sleeping in Sunday mornings
the gap never
wider than five points
such satisfaction in symmetry

So when I demonstrate
a one-two on your shoulder—
soft as a sparrow landing
one foot then the other—
you startle at confrontation,
seep toward the door

I know I've upended our balance,
don't want to bully,
but my fists have been taught
to feed on the fear
in your flailing palms

friday night fights

Ten o'clock yawning
heavy on the couch,
watching the real boxers on TV
prancing in their tasselled shorts,
pumping gloves at the crowd
as the announcer stretches
their names like taffy

At the bell, I look for an opening,
kick at your thigh for more room
but you're quick to parry, block

The boxers bounce drumroll punches
off taut muscle, bob like buoys
I work the angles,
chip away at your defence

After twelve rounds, a decision
but my win undeniable
as I unfurl ragged legs
across your defeated lap

expectation

You knew I wasn't
all smiles, sunshine,
kittens and lip gloss

That I'd never be a woman
who'd play at princess,
wilt as wife

You didn't expect satin gloves
smoothed to the elbow,
but neither ten ounce leather
or their stench

Never boxing

Even though I've always pulled
toward the tight groove of discipline,
the far side of expectation
and loved looking at your face
with the word *surprise*
tickling my tongue

Still, you'd planned
to spend years watching me
read, sip tea, scratch at poems
about birds and kisses
never guessed fighting would muscle in
to our dinner conversations,
Sunday mornings, all the little tucks
and gathers of our lives

You won't say you're proud
or that the thought of me
in the ring turns you on
but I know from recurring dreams
the wonder of opening a cupboard door,
discovering a new world
inside a home whose every inch
you've touched, loved thoroughly

muscle

I strain with you
against you
with you
in the dark
like the exchange
of jab and counter
daring and defence

Your hands drift
from my breasts to biceps
their new contour
firm conviction
a stranger in our bed

I feel the thrill
flicker through your fingers
echo in your breath

photo

You watch every round
through the viewfinder
lens filters, shrinks punches

On a tiny screen
the fight could be cute
instead of trading blows,
I might be placing a cookie
in her mouth, letting her
pat my face in thanks

You try again and again
to hold me safe
with the pinch
of shutter

SIX MINUTES

uppercut

*Arm a crescent of muscle,
drop and dig
power from your belly*

*Thrust to ceiling,
relentless as a geyser*

dual/duel

Brain, the hero,
the smug, swaggering alpha,
thinks a fight
is philosophical argument

Body, its tag-along,
bumbling sidekick,
knows better

⊙

Brain relishes the sport
of conflict
straight-A member
of the debate team,
can fight out of either corner

Body frowns,
frets about damage, failure

⊙

In the ring,
Brain is lean and trash-talking,
arrogant, pish-poshing
two-minute rounds
hardly enough to bother gloving up

Body quakes,
electric tremble through fingernails

☉

Bell rings
Brain whirls,
realizes cleverness isn't enough
under attack that might as well
be machine-gun fire

Body understands its job:
scans muscle for cache of strength
becomes machinery,
manufactures blows

☉

Brain cowers,
would turn and run,
hand over the win
anything to return to its cushioned chair,
a book left open

Body works hard,
stoic as a character in a fairy tale

☉

After,
Brain chastened, humble,
shakes hands with Body

Body doesn't gloat,
just flexes biceps
as the win storms
through blood stream

weight class

From across the gym
coach asks my weight
like it's a shoe size or address,
the kind of question
a woman could answer
in a crowded room

But I'm used to
the indignities of the ring,
flaws in my body,
its operation

I've learned not to flinch
even as I say *one-forty*
out loud

commitment

I waited

For my body to balk,
retreat to safety

For coach
to touch my elbow
in the locker room,
suggest yoga, golf

For a broken rib,
sprained wrist
for a sudden drop in weight
to curdle the match

But nothing decided
I shouldn't fight

locker room

We fuss over wrapped hands,
bounce to the beat of nerves,
muffled Metallica throb

She leans into the mirror,
tucks hair under a bandana,
says *this feels like getting married*
and we laugh at bouquets
clutched in boxing gloves,
bridesmaids in silk trunks

But truth balloons inside the joke
as we solemnly walk down the aisle
expecting to be transformed by a ring,
by vows we've made to ourselves

silence

They hollered last fight,
whooped at blood,
thump of body blows

Now I hear fizzy sips of beer,
every wince and fidget
programs folded, unfolded
until paper frays

We bash at silence,
read respect or disapproval
in the stunned hush
of two hundred people
watching women in the ring

six minutes

Round 1

Bell tears a hole in my gut
confidence drops through
whole and heavy,
bomb from the belly of a plane

I tiptoe to centre ring,
shyly bump gloves, wait
for arms to remember,
recite one-twos
long, straight punches
to every listening inch of her face

She hits me a dozen times
before denting my adrenalin

Steady, strong,
I jot neat, iambic lines
on her forehead, precise as a typist

Opposite arms of a compass,
we circle
circle
circle
one another
until the bell shatters
our measured breath

Round 2

I try to hide
the nick in my energy,
slight stutter of lungs
but she sees the gap,
picks away at my stitching

My focus threadbare,
more tattered with every punch
I take to the face

I see past her,
beyond the ring:
empty chair beside my husband,
the beer waiting damp in his hand

She inches me to the ropes,
explodes with throws
I become the door
she must break down
to save her child

In the fluster of gloves
I find my left hand,
one jab inside it

Enough to widen her eyes,
get her into range
of my right
a cross so heavy
it snaps her head back—
exaggerated agreement
with the way I've folded her nose
into her face

Round 3

In my corner they warn
she's behind on points,
will come out mean at the bell

I see—in her shoulders,
her focus—she wants the win
more

I throw and throw,
dig a hole large enough to hide in
one hundred and twenty
breathless seconds
until the bell
calls truce

I pant in my corner
someone undoes gloves,
pops out mouthguard

Ref pulls me back
to centre ring,
lifts my long, long, heavy arm
to the ceiling

win

I don't have the breath, the gall
to howl in the locker room

Just inch jeans up sticky legs, towel hair,
realize how small the win is
beside the idea of the fight

I watch the rest of the card with one eye—
the other focused inside my skin,
trying to pinpoint what has changed

replay

I was serene
as I commanded fists
to explode fast and bright
as firecrackers
in her face

Tall, steady, I led
her around the ring,
watched from above
as she tiptoed up to reach

I intercepted every punch,
slipped nimbly
listened to her glove break the air
beside my left ear, then the right

But now, watching the replay on screen,
I cringe at my stiff lope,
my anxious, lanky arms
throwing at faces in the crowd
and gasp at all the punches
I inhaled through the nose

naming

Someone says *fighter*
and I look
over my shoulder
for the boxer behind me

I can't claim that title
after three little rounds
in old runners

My eyes have never purpled,
puffed shut
my nose still long,
straight as my mother's

I know I don't deserve
that word, just like I slipped
from *poet* until I saw my name
on a thin black spine

But gloved fists say *fighter*
just like words
stacked flush left mean *poem*
no matter how clumsily
they've been placed

after

I thought I'd sleep,
wake relieved
never think again of fighting

But the days after fit poorly,
plain, aimless
without the thrill of the ring

Muscles regress,
leave me with photos, trophy
a story I'll write sometime

For weeks, I hug the pain, the pride,
that flashes between ribs

Many thanks to:

All the good people at Pan Am Boxing, especially Lisa, Harry, Sue, Kevin, Dennis, Rose and everyone involved in the March, 2009 white collar fights. Extra thanks to Lisa for supportive coaching and guidance, both in the ring and in these pages.

The 2009 May Day poets, especially Ariel Gordon, and the Banff Centre's fall 2009 Writing with Style poets for your feedback and for never saying "*another* poem about boxing?"

The Manitoba Arts Council, for supporting the development of this project.

Jeanette Lynes for calling this a book before it was one, and Robert Kroetsch for lending me kind words.

Brian and Karen at Anvil Press—I'm so pleased to be part of your team.

Friends and family, especially those who didn't question the boxing. (And those of you who did, for your care and concern.)

And, of course, Jeope—for the cover art, and every other little thing.